IN THE ARMS OF HIS LOVE

GORDON B. HINCKLEY

DESERET
BOOK

Salt Lake City, Utah

ISBN-13   978-1-59038-705-4

Printed in the United States of America
Artistic Printing, Salt Lake City, Utah

10   9   8   7   6   5   4   3   2

A friend not of our faith once said to me, "LDS stands for Love, Devotion, Service." What does Relief Society really stand for? What does it mean? Let me try to say something about this.

Relief Society stands for Love. What a remarkable thing it is to witness the love of good women one for another. They mingle together in the bonds of love with friendship and respect for each other. This organization is actually the only resource that many women have for friendly association.

It is the natural instinct of women to reach out in love to those in distress and need. The welfare program of the Church is described as priesthood based, but it could not function without the Relief Society.

Relief Society stands for Education. It is the obligation of every woman of this Church to get all the education she can. It will enlarge her life and increase her opportunities. It will provide her with marketable skills in case she needs them.

Recently I received a letter from a single mother, a part of which I wish to share with you. She says as follows:

"It has been 10 years since you mentioned our family in October conference in 1996. . . . The words of counsel and encouragement that you gave to me and other single sisters have been a pattern used in my daily life. The phrase that has become my motto and watchword [is] 'Do the very best you can,' and that is indeed what my sons and I are trying to do.

"All four of my sons graduated from high school and seminary. Two of them served full-time missions. We are all working to provide for ourselves and continue to be true and faithful in the gospel. It is a great feeling to know that we have made it on our own for the past several years. . . . There is a certain feeling of accomplishment when you can once again stand on your own two feet and provide for your family's needs. . . .

"I was encouraged to go back to college. . . . It is a

real challenge to work full-time and attend classes at night. It has broadened my perspective on life and helped me to be a better person. My family, ward members, and co-workers have been very supportive. I will graduate this December.

"As I pondered my patriarchal blessing and made it a matter of fasting and prayer, I was able to set some realistic goals in my life that have been used as a road map to keep me on track with the principles of the gospel. I attend my meetings, pray daily, and pay my tithing. I . . . take my calling as a visiting teacher very seriously. . . .

"The Church is true, and it is an honor and a privilege to be counted as a worthy and blessed member of The Church of Jesus Christ of Latter-day Saints. We are led by inspiration from a loving Heavenly Father, who knows us and wants us to progress and grow. I thank you for your kind words of encouragement 10 years ago, and for the many continuing words of inspiration that come from the Lord through His servants. I know I am a child of God and my life is blessed by my membership in His Church."

Relief Society stands for Self-reliance. The best food storage is not in welfare grain elevators but in sealed cans and bottles in the homes of our people. What a gratifying thing it is to see cans of wheat and rice and beans under the beds or in the pantries of women who have taken welfare responsibility into their own hands. Such food may not be tasty, but it will be nourishing if it has to be used.

Relief Society means Sacrifice. I am always moved by this simple verse of Anne Campbell, written in behalf of her child. Said she:

> *You are the trip I did not take;*
> *You are the pearls I cannot buy;*
> *You are my blue Italian lake;*
> *You are my piece of foreign sky.*

("To My Child," quoted in Charles L. Wallis, ed., *The Treasure Chest* [1965], 54.)

Many of you are mothers. You are responsible for the nurture and upbringing of your children. When you grow old and your hair turns white, you will not ask about the fancy clothes you once wore, the cars you drove, or the large house in which you lived. Your burning question will be, "How have my children turned out?"

If they have turned out well, you will be grateful.

If otherwise, there will be only small consolation for you.

I have written elsewhere: "God bless you, mothers. When all the victories and defeats of men's efforts are tallied, when the dust of life's battles begins to settle, when all for which we labor so hard in this world of conquest fades before our eyes, you will be there, you must be there, as the strength for a new generation, the ever-improving onward movement of the race" (*One Bright Shining Hope* [Salt Lake City: Deseret Book, 2006], 18).

Some years ago in the Salt Lake Tabernacle, Elder Marion D. Hanks conducted a panel discussion. Included in that panel was an attractive and able young woman, divorced, the mother of seven children then ranging in ages from 7 to 16. She said that one evening she went across the street to deliver something to a neighbor. Listen to her words, as I recall them:

"As I turned around to walk back home, I could see my house lighted up. I could hear echoes of my children as I had walked out of the door a few minutes earlier. They were saying: 'Mom, what are we going to have for dinner?' 'Can you take me to the library?' 'I have to get some poster paper tonight.' Tired and weary, I looked at that house and saw the light on in each of the rooms. I thought of all of those children who were home waiting for me to come and meet their needs. My burdens felt heavier than I could bear.

"I remember looking through tears toward the sky, and I said, 'Dear Father, I just can't do it tonight. I'm too tired. I can't face it. I can't go home and take care of all those children alone. Could I just come to You and stay with You for just one night? I'll come back in the morning.'

"I didn't really hear the words of reply, but I heard them in my mind. The answer was: 'No, little one, you can't come to me now. You would never wish to come back. But I can come to you.'"

There are so very many like this young mother, who found herself in loneliness and desperation but was fortunate enough to have faith in the Lord, who could love her and help her.

Relief Society means Faith. It means putting first things first. It means such a thing as the payment of tithing.

Elder Lynn Robbins of the Seventy tells this story of a stake president from Panama.

As a young man recently returned from his mission,

he found the girl he wanted to marry. They were happy, but very poor.

Then came a particularly difficult time when their food and money ran out. It was a Saturday, and the cupboard was literally bare. Rene felt distraught that his young wife was hungry. He decided he had no other choice than to use their tithing money and go purchase food.

As he was leaving the house, his wife stopped him and asked him where he was going. He told her he was going to buy food. She asked him where he got the money. He told her that it was the tithing money. She said, "That is the Lord's money—you will not use that to buy food." Her faith was stronger than his. He put the money back, and they went to bed hungry that night.

The next morning they had no breakfast, and they went to church fasting. Rene gave the tithing money to the bishop, but he was too proud to tell the bishop that they were in need.

After the meetings he and his wife left the chapel and started to walk home. They hadn't gone very far when a new member called to them from his house. This man was a fisherman and told them he had more fish than he could use. He wrapped five little fish in a newspaper for them, and they thanked him. As they continued to walk home, they were stopped by another member who gave them tortillas; then someone else stopped them and gave them rice; another member saw them and gave them beans.

When they arrived home, they had enough food for two weeks. They were even more surprised when they unwrapped the package of fish and found two very large fish and not the five smaller ones they thought they had seen. They cut the fish in portions and stored it in their neighbor's freezer.

They have repeatedly testified that never since then have they gone hungry.

My dear sisters, all of these wonderful qualities which Relief Society stands for represent being encircled eternally in the arms of His love.

It is this for which we all wish. It is this for which we all hope. It is this for which we all pray.

Now, just a word in conclusion. I remind you that you are not second-class citizens in the kingdom of God. You are His divine creation. Men hold the priesthood. Yours is a different role, but also extremely important. Without you, our Father's plan of happiness would be frustrated and have no real meaning. You are 50 percent of the membership of the Church and mothers of the other 50 percent. No one can dismiss you lightly.

I once received a letter from a dear friend. Her name is Helen, and her husband's name is Charlie. She writes as follows, among other things:

"Today Charlie and I spoke at our sacrament meeting. In my talk I related the advice you gave me when I graduated from Idaho Falls High School and had made plans to attend Ricks College. You told me that I should attend the Church College of Hawaii, where I would have a better chance to meet and marry a young man of Chinese ancestry.

"I took your advice and went to CCH, where I met Charlie and married him. We have been married 37 years and have five children. All of our five children have served missions. . . . Three of our children married in the Hawaiian temple. We have two single children, and we hope they will find worthy individuals to take to the temple soon. We have six adorable grandchildren and two more on the way.

"I have been blessed to have a faithful husband who honors his priesthood and has been worthy to serve the Lord as bishop, stake president, and mission president. It has been my privilege to support him in all his Church assignments. I have served as stake Relief Society president for almost five years.

"Today, as I count my many blessings, I could not help but think of what a great influence you have been in my life. I just want you to know that I followed your counsel, and because of that my life has been blessed abundantly. I thank you for taking the time to follow my progress when I left Hong Kong to come to America."

This is what the Relief Society does for women. It gives them opportunity for growth and development. It gives them status as queens in their own households. It gives them place and position, where they grow as they exercise their talents. It gives them pride and direction in family life. It gives them added appreciation for good, eternal companions and children.

There is nothing to compare with it in all the world.